TABLE OF CONTENTS

The most dangerous animals in the world belong to many different groups: mammals, fish, reptiles, insects, and arachnids. Not all of them are predators, but even the ones that are usually gentle can be driven to deadly attacks on people.

AFRICAN ELEPHANT

The African elephant is the largest animal on land. These intelligent plant eaters aren't dangerous when left alone, but conflicts between humans and elephants can lead to deadly attacks.

When Elephants Attack

Elephants are typically peaceful animals, but they can be deadly when defending themselves, their young, or their territories. During mating season, older male elephants go into musth (pronounced "must"), and they become very aggressive and dangerous. Elephants attack other animals and humans by charging—as fast as 30 mph (48 kph)—goring with their tusks, trampling, and swinging their trunks with deadly force. As humans take away more elephant habitat and harm more animals, elephants attack more often. African and Asian elephants together kill about 500 people every year.

WORLD'S MOST DANGEROUS ANIMALS

By Paul Beck

SCHOLASTIC

an imprint of
SCHOLASTIC
www.scholastic.com

Copyright © 2012 becker&mayer! LLC

Published by Tangerine Press, an imprint of Scholastic Inc.,
557 Broadway, New York, NY 10012
Scholastic Canada Ltd., Markham, Ontario
Scholastic Australia Pty. Ltd, Gosford NSW
Scholastic New Zealand Ltd., Greenmount, Auckland

becker&mayer!
BOOK PRODUCERS

Produced by becker&mayer!
11120 NE 33rd Place, Suite 101
Bellevue, WA 98004

www.beckermayer.com

If you have questions or comments about this product, please visit www.beckermayer.com/customerservice and click on Customer Service Request Form.

Edited by Ben Grossblatt
Designed by Rosanna Brockley
3-D anaglyph effects by Brandon Walker and Thumbprints Utd Holdings Pte Ltd.
Production management by Tom Miller
Photo research by Katie del Rosario

Photo credits:
Title page: Snarling wolf © Keith Szafranski/iStockphoto. Page 4: African elephant charging © Uryadnikov Sergey/Shutterstock. Page 5: Elephant stampede © Anup Shah/Photolibrary; elephant spraying © Anup Shah/Nature Picture Library. Page 6: Bengal tiger snarling © Lu2006/Dreamstime. Page 7: Tiger fight © Anup Shah/Nature Picture Library; tiger leaping © J-L. Klein & M-L. Hubert/Photolibrary. Page 8: Black widow spider © John Cancalosi/Peter Arnold Images/Photolibrary. Page 9: Black widow with egg sac © Barh CM/Photolibrary; black widow on branch © Mark Kostich/iStockphoto. Page 10: Cape buffalo © Peter Betts/Shutterstock. Page 11: Cape buffalo horns © Anup Shah/Nature Picture Library; cape buffalo fight © Claude Balcaen/Photolibrary. Page 12: Angry chimpanzee © Michael Elliott/Dreamstime. Page 13: Chimpanzee in tree © Noppadon Chanruangdecha/Dreamstime; chimpanzees waiting © Michel Gunther/Photolibrary. Page 14: Deathstalker scorpion © Batonchik/Dreamstime. Page 15: Scorpion with babies © Ivan Kuzmin/Imagebroker.net/Photolibrary; scorpion © Kennan Ward/Nomad/Photolibrary. Page 16: Gray wolf snarling © David Welling/Nature Picture Library. Page 17: Wolf pack © Gea Strucks/Dreamstime; wolves howling © Alexey Shulika/Dreamstime. Page 18: Great white shark © Firefly Productions/Flirt Collection/Photolibrary. Page 19: Shark mouth © Photomyeye/Dreamstime; shark attack © Vnoucek F/Photolibrary. Page 20: Grizzly bear © Seread/Dreamstime. Page 21: Bear growling © Alexander Sukonkin/Dreamstime; bear fight © BostjanT/iStockphoto. Page 22: Hippopotamus © tratong/Shutterstock. Page 23: Group of hippos © Blaine Harrington/Age fotostock/Photolibrary; hippo fight © Graeme Shannon/Shutterstock. Page 24: Running jaguar © PureStock/Photolibrary. Page 25: Snarling jaguar © Carol Farneti Foster/Oxford Scientific/Photolibrary; jaguar confrontation © Sharon Morris/Shutterstock. Page 26: King cobra © DV/Photolibrary. Page 27: Cobra hissing © Omar Ariff Kamarul Ariffin/Dreamstime; back of cobra © Dinodia Dinodia/Aflo Photo Agency/Photolibrary. Page 28: Komodo dragon © Gerard Fritz/Nordic Photos/Photolibrary. Page 29: Komodo dragons charging © Pius Lee/Shutterstock; komodo dragons eating © Reinhard Dirscherl/WaterFrame – Underwater Images/Photolibrary. Page 30: Lion snarling © Kristian Sekulic/iStockphoto. Page 31: Lioness hunting © Carl Winberg/iStockphoto; lioness confrontation © Jean-Jacques Alcalay/Photolibrary. Page 32: Mosaic eel © Ross Armstrong/Age fotostock/Photolibrary. Page 33: Green eel © David Safanda/iStockphoto; giant moray eel with diver © Gerard Fritz/Nordic Photo/Photolibrary. Page 34: Mosquito © Henrik Larsson/iStockphoto. Page 35: Mosquito biting © Dmitry Knorre/Dreamstime; mosquito with eggs © Douglas Allen/iStockphoto. Page 36: Nile crocodile hunting © Sergey Uryadnikov/Dreamstime. Page 37: Crocodile jaw © Steve Allen/Dreamstime; group of crocs © Trevor Kelly/Dreamstime. Page 38: Orangutan © Corbis/Photolibrary. Page 39: Angry orangutan © Sergey Uryadnikov/Dreamstime; orangutan in tree © Csaba Vanyi/Dreamstime. Page 40: Polar bear © Kennan Ward/Nomad/Photolibrary. Page 41: Polar bear leaping © Andy Rousse/Nature Picture Library; polar bear fight © Shutterstock. Page 42: Spotted hyenas © Anup Shah/Nature Picture Library. Page 43: Hyena running © Paul Banton/Dreamstime; group of hyenas © Stefanie Van Der Vinden/Dreamstime. Page 44: Western diamondback rattlesnake © Audrey Snider-Bell/Shutterstock. Page 45: Western diamondback ready to strike © Brian Lasenby/Shutterstock; diamondback warning rattle © Steve Byland/Dreamstime. Page 46: Wolverine © Daniel Cox/Oxford Scientific/Photolibrary. Page 47: Wolverine snarling © Justin Kral/iStockphoto; wolverine stalking © Geoffrey Kuchera/Shutterstock.

TP4523-1 11/11
Printed, manufactured, and assembled in Dongguan, China

10 9 8 7 6 5 4 3 2 1
ISBN: 978-0-545-42491-2
Conforms to ASTM standard F963-08 and CPSIA.

11830

If one charging elephant is dangerous, an elephant stampede is off the scale.

THAT'S WILD

SCIENTIFIC NAME:
Loxodonta africana

LENGTH: 25 ft. (7.6 m)

HEIGHT: 13 ft. (4 m)

WEIGHT: 7 tons (6.4 t)

LOCATION: southern and central Africa

Handy Trunk

An elephant's trunk can do nearly everything a human hand can do, and more. It can pick up objects as large as a tree trunk or as small as a blade of grass. It can spray water, too. The elephant also uses its trunk to communicate, by sound and touch, and to smell things. (It's a nose, after all.) The trunk can even be a weapon.

BENGAL TIGER

The tiger is the biggest member of the cat family. More than half of all wild tigers are Bengal tigers. Tigers hunt large mammals like deer and wild pigs. In areas where human activity has taken away tiger habitat and food, the big cats may prey on livestock or even people.

ENDANGERED

Tigers have the longest canine teeth of any predator on land. The teeth can measure up to 3 inches (7.6 cm) in length, as long as a human middle finger.

Tigers usually avoid other tigers, but sometimes fights break out. Tiger fights are rarely fatal.

Striped Tiger

Tigers hunt by stealth and surprise, either waiting in ambush or silently stalking an unsuspecting deer or pig. The striped coat makes the tiger nearly invisible in tall grass or trees. With a rush and a leap, the tiger slams into its prey and drags it to the ground with 4-inch (10-cm) claws. A bite to the neck kills smaller prey. With larger prey, the tiger clamps its canine teeth on the animal's windpipe until it suffocates.

A Siberian tiger springs from the snow.

A running tiger can hit a top speed of 35 mph (56 kph), but it can't keep that pace up for very long. When stalking or waiting in ambush, the tiger needs to be within 100 feet (30.5 m) of its prey before charging.

THAT'S WILD

SCIENTIFIC NAME: *Panthera tigris tigris*

LENGTH: 9 ft. (2.7 m), nose to tail

WEIGHT: up to 400 lbs. (181 kg)

LOCATION: India, Nepal, Bhutan, and Bangladesh

BLACK WIDOW SPIDER

Drop for drop, a black widow spider's venom is more powerful than that of a rattlesnake. Luckily for humans, this spider is shy and will bite a person only in self-defense. Its bite causes swelling, muscle pain, and temporary paralysis, but usually not death. Still, the venom is fatal to one out of every 25 people bitten.

Dangerous Females

Only female black widows are dangerous to humans. They are shiny black or sometimes brown, with a red hourglass shape on their undersides. Males are smaller and lighter brown.

Young black widows also have colored marks on their backs.

Bug Killer

Whether or not a black widow's bite is fatal to humans, it's certain death for the spider's prey. The black widow waits in hiding by its web until a fly, beetle, or other insect gets trapped in the sticky mesh. The spider rushes out, imprisons its prey in a cocoon of silk, then punctures the insect with its fangs and injects the deadly venom.

Watch Out

People are most likely to come across black widows in places like the corners of basements, barns, and garages. Before indoor plumbing, many black widow bites happened when the victim accidentally sat on the spider in the outhouse.

THAT'S WILD

SCIENTIFIC NAME:
Latrodectus mactans

SIZE: 1.5 in. (3.8 cm)

LOCATION: every continent except Antarctica

CAPE BUFFALO

The Cape buffalo is a wild African cousin of the domestic cow. But it's a bigger and much more dangerous cousin. Cape buffalo are famous for their short tempers and deadly 5-foot (1.5-m) horns.

This is a view of a Cape buffalo you don't want to see. Bulls can charge as fast as 35mph (56 kph) over short distances.

THAT'S WILD

SCIENTIFIC NAME: *Syncerus caffer caffer*

LENGTH: 11 ft. (3.4 m)

HEIGHT: 5.5 ft. (1.7 m)

WEIGHT: 2,000 lbs. (900 kg)

LOCATION: much of Southern Africa

Armed with Horns

A Cape buffalo's main weapons are its gigantic horns. Both males and females have them. The male's horns widen and flatten at the base to form a helmet-like shield, called a boss, on the buffalo's forehead. Each curved horn can be as long as 5 feet (1.5 m). Males spar with their horns when competing for mates. These contests are like rituals rather than real fights. But buffalo won't hesitate to use their horns as deadly weapons to protect themselves and others in the herd from predators. There are many stories of big game hunters being gored to death and even tossed into trees by angry Cape buffalo.

Two aggressive Cape buffalo in Kenya.

CHIMPANZEE

Chimpanzees are large, strong, and very smart. Chimps in the wild aren't usually dangerous to humans, though there have been some cases of attacks. The problem comes when people try to keep chimpanzees as pets. Chimps, especially males, can be aggressive. "Pet" chimpanzees have been known to attack with hands, feet, and teeth, causing serious injuries.

Chimpanzees have very big, sharp teeth. Chimps in captivity have been known to bite fingers off of unwary humans whose hands get too close. Unlike smiling humans, chimpanzees bare their teeth to show fear and aggression.

Chimpanzees have strong arm muscles for climbing.
They are twice as strong as humans.

THAT'S WILD

SCIENTIFIC NAME: *Pan troglodytes*
HEIGHT: 4 ft. (1.2 m)
WEIGHT: 120 lbs. (54 kg)
LOCATION: near the Equator in Africa

Chimp Communities

Chimpanzees live together in groups of about 50 apes, called communities. Within the community there are smaller family groups. Sometimes a gang of chimps from one community will attack and even kill apes from a neighboring community. Scientists don't know whether the attackers are after more territory or mates. Though they are mostly vegetarian, chimpanzees also hunt and eat animals, including monkeys. Chimps use their teeth and hands for both killing and tearing apart their prey. Recently, scientists discovered a group of chimps using spearlike tools for hunting.

DEATHSTALKER SCORPION

Scorpions are arachnids (uh-RACK-nids), in the same large group of animals that includes spiders and ticks. When it comes to scorpions, the smaller and more slender, the deadlier. The slender, pale yellow deathstalker has one of the strongest venoms of all scorpions.

The general rule about scorpions: Scorpions with smaller pincers tend to have deadlier venom.

THAT'S WILD

SCIENTIFIC NAME: *Leiurus quinquestriatus*

SIZE: 4 in. (10 cm)

LOCATION: deserts of northern Africa and the Middle East

All Aboard!

Scorpions give birth to live young. After the babies emerge, they ride around on their mother's back for several weeks until they are large enough to go off on their own.

Offensive Weapon

The scorpion's stinger is at the tip of its tail. When a scorpion attacks, it whips its tail forward over its body to deliver an injection of powerful venom. The venom is a neurotoxin (NURR-oh-tocks-in), meaning that it affects the nervous system. Scorpions hunt by detecting vibrations made by the prey as it moves along the ground. Scorpions use their stingers as offensive weapons to kill or paralyze prey, but they only sting humans and large animals in self-defense. Of the 1,500 scorpion species in the world, only about 25 can kill humans. The death stalker is one of them.

GRAY WOLF

Wolves are pack hunters with a fearsome reputation. They're not usually a threat to humans, but they're deadly to deer, elk, moose, and other prey animals.

Like dogs and humans, wolves communicate with their faces.
The message on this wolf's face is obvious: "Back off!"

THAT'S WILD

SCIENTIFIC NAME: *Canis lupus*

SIZE: 6 ft. (1.8 m), nose to tail

WEIGHT: 175 lbs. (79 kg)

LOCATION: northern North America, eastern Europe, and Russia

Pack Life

Wolves live and hunt together in packs with as few as two and as many as 12 members. The pack is usually based around a breeding pair of wolves, along with their current cubs and the young from the year before. Sometimes an unrelated wolf will also belong to the pack. The leader, called the alpha male, is the male of the breeding pair. The pack hunts together, ranging over great distances. The wolves work as a group to chase down and kill large animals like caribou or moose. A single wolf can eat as much as 20 pounds (9 kg) of meat in one meal.

Howling

Wolves communicate in many different ways, but the most well-known is howling. A wolf howls by itself when it gets separated from the pack to let the others know where it is. Wolves howl together to find other packs and warn them away from their territory. They may even howl together simply because they like doing it.

GREAT WHITE SHARK

With awesome speed, super senses, and jaws that can crunch through even a sea turtle's shell, the great white shark is the biggest predator of all fish. This hunter can smell blood in the water and rush to the attack from 3 miles (5 km) away.

The great white shark is streamlined like a torpedo, with a top speed of 15 mph (24 kph).

Razor Mouth

A great white's mouth is lined with large, supersharp triangular teeth. Their edges are serrated like steak knives. The mouth has several rows of teeth. When one tooth falls out, another moves into its place from the row behind.

Shark Attack!

Great white sharks often attack with a surprise rush from below. If the first razor-toothed chomp doesn't take care of the victim right away, the prey usually dies very soon from blood loss. But sometimes the bite is off the mark, and the prey escapes with nondeadly injuries. Young great whites eat other fish. As the sharks grow, they move on to mammals, like seals, sea lions, and even smaller members of the whale family, such as porpoises. In the whole world, there are about 30 great white shark attacks on humans every year, but most aren't fatal.

THAT'S WILD

SCIENTIFIC NAME: *Carcharadon carcharias*

SIZE: 20 ft. (6 m)

WEIGHT: 2.5 tons (2.3 t)

LOCATION: coastal waters around the world

19

GRIZZLY BEAR

More than 80 percent of a grizzly bear's diet is plants, but in the diet of a quarter-ton (230 kg) animal, that still leaves room for plenty of meat. Grizzlies eat animals of all types and sizes, from insect grubs to deer, caribou, and moose. It's especially dangerous for humans to come between a bear and its kill or a mother and her cubs.

THAT'S WILD

SCIENTIFIC NAME: *Ursus arctos horribilis*

SIZE: 7 ft. (2 m) tall when standing

WEIGHT: 600 lbs. (270 kg)

LOCATION: northern North America

Grizzly vs. Black Bear

Grizzly bears are also called brown bears, but their color ranges from light brown to almost black. Some grizzlies' fur looks frosted, or grizzled, which gives this animal its name. To tell a grizzly bear from the smaller and less dangerous black bear, look for the concave (inward) curve on top of the snout, the huge, muscled hump on the shoulders, and the long, knifelike claws. Grizzlies are also larger than black bears. Males can weigh more than 600 pounds (270 kg). But that doesn't mean the grizzly is a slow, lumbering beast. A running grizzly can clock in at more than 35 mph (56 kph), fast enough to cross a football field in less than six seconds and more than fast enough to chase down even the speediest human.

Brawls

Grizzlies spend most of their time alone, foraging and hunting for food. During mating season, males fight each other to compete for mates.

HIPPOPOTAMUS

The hippopotamus may be a vegetarian, but it's one of the most dangerous animals in Africa. In the water, an aggressive hippo can capsize a boat with ease, drowning or even chomping its occupants with enormous teeth. On land, a charging hippopotamus can smash into you with the power of a tank.

Giant Teeth

The hippo's dagger-sharp canine teeth keep growing throughout the animal's life. They can reach lengths of 20 inches (51 cm). When the hippo closes its mouth, the giant lower teeth fit into sheaths in the upper jaw. Males use their canines to fight with each other over territory.

THAT'S WILD

SCIENTIFIC NAME: *Hippopotamus amphibius*

SIZE: 15 feet (4.6 m) long, 5 feet (1.5 m) tall at the shoulder

WEIGHT: 3 tons (2.7 t) for males, 1.5 tons (1.4 t) for females

LOCATION: sub-Saharan Africa

To a hippopotamus, a big yawn means, "Go away, or I'll attack!"

Male hippos fight to defend their territory.

River Horse

Hippos spend most of the day in the water, wallowing in the shallows or walking along the bottom of deeper areas in graceful slow motion. (*Hippopotamus* means "river horse.") Although it can't swim, a hippopotamus can hold its breath underwater for as long as five minutes. In the evening, hippos come onto land to graze on grasses and other plants.

JAGUAR

The jaguar is the largest cat in the Americas and the third largest in the world, smaller only than the tiger and lion. Jaguars are skilled swimmers and climbers. They sometimes pounce on prey from the branches of a tree.

Jaguars are good swimmers. They usually live near streams, rivers, swamps, and other watery areas.

THAT'S WILD

SCIENTIFIC NAME: *Panthera onca*

SIZE: 7 ft. (2 m), nose to tail

WEIGHT: 300 lbs. (135 kg)

LOCATION: Central and South America

Teeth

Jaguars kill their large prey with a bite through the back of the skull. The jaws and canine teeth are powerful and sharp enough to puncture bone. They can even bite through turtle shells. Jaguars like to hunt large animals, such as deer, tapirs, wild pigs, and the giant rodents called capybaras. But they will eat anything they can catch, including reptiles, mammals, birds, fish, and even (rarely) people.

Jaguar or Leopard?

Jaguars and leopards look similar, but it's easy to spot the difference: The black ring patterns on a jaguar's coat, called rosettes, often have spots in the middle. A leopard's rosettes never do. Jaguars are also stockier and more muscular. And, easiest of all, if it's in the Americas, it's a jaguar. If it's in Africa, it's a leopard.

Even black jaguars—sometimes called panthers—have rosettes. They're darker black against a black fur background and can be hard to see.

25

KING COBRA

The king cobra is the largest venomous snake in the world. One bite from a king cobra can inject enough venom to kill an elephant. Luckily, this snake is shy and usually avoids humans. But a cornered cobra isn't shy at all about defending itself, and a female guarding her eggs can attack without warning.

A king cobra can raise as much as one-third of its body off the ground. That's high enough for it to look a human in the eye.

Living Like Royalty

King cobras' habitat includes rain forests, plains, and swamps. King cobras mostly hunt and eat other snakes, but they will also eat lizards, rodents, and other small mammals. King cobras are the only snakes that build nests. The female lays her eggs in a nest built of sticks and leaves, and then sits on top of the nest to guard them. Nesting females are especially aggressive and dangerous. King cobras don't have the strongest venom of all snakes, but their bite delivers a huge dose.

When threatened, the cobra rears up and spreads its familiar hood. The snake will also open its mouth and give a warning hiss. It's a good idea to pay attention to the warning.

THAT'S WILD

SCIENTIFIC NAME:
Ophiophagus hannah

SIZE: 18 ft. (5.5 m)

WEIGHT: 20 lbs. (9 kg)

LOCATION: southeast Asia, southern China, and northeast India

KOMODO DRAGON

The Komodo dragon is the largest, most dangerous lizard in the world. Komodo dragons have the speed and power to bring down prey as large as a water buffalo. They're also the only lizards known to have killed and eaten people.

Like other reptiles, the Komodo dragon smells with its tongue and a sense organ in the roof of its mouth called the Jacobson's organ. If the wind is right, the lizard can detect prey up to 5 miles (8 km) away.

THAT'S WILD

SCIENTIFIC NAME: *Varanus komodoensis*

SIZE: 10 ft. (3 m)

WEIGHT: 175 lbs. (79 kg)

LOCATION: small islands of Indonesia

Deadly Lizard

Komodo dragons have powerful legs and strong, sharp claws. They can run as fast as 11 mph (18 kph) for short distances. They use their claws to attack and hold prey. The dragon's mouth is filled with 60 razor-sharp teeth. These lizards are venomous, and their saliva is chock full of dangerous bacteria.

Cannibals!

Except during breeding season, Komodo dragons don't spend much time with one another. There's a good reason: they're cannibals. As much as one-tenth of a Komodo dragon's diet is other, smaller Komodo dragons. In fact, young Komodo dragons spend the first several years of their lives living in trees. It gives them a better chance of not being eaten.

LION

Lions are powerful hunters capable of taking down large prey. Lions live in groups called prides. Each pride has as many as 30 lions. Of those, most are females, called lionesses. Female cubs usually stay in the same pride as their mothers, but about one-third will leave to join other prides. Males leave their pride by the time they're about four years old.

Guarding Their Turf

A pride of lions might live in the same territory for generations and will protect its turf against invaders. A male lion's roar can be a threatening signal for lions from outside the pride to stay away.

A lion's roar can be heard more than 3 miles (5 km) away.

THAT'S WILD

SCIENTIFIC NAME: *Panthera leo*

LENGTH: 10 ft. (3 m) long, nose to tail

WEIGHT: 550 lbs. (250 kg)

LOCATION: African grasslands and the Gir Forest of India

Pack Living, Solo Hunting

Lions are the only cats that live in social groups. Lionesses take care of cubs together, and they work together to hunt large prey, but lions usually hunt smaller prey by themselves.

Although lions live in communities, fights can break out.

MORAY EEL

With their long, thin bodies and their lack of legs or fins, eels resemble snakes. But eels are actually an order of fish with about 800 species. The family of moray eels contains about 200 species, and moray eels can be identified by their eyes set far forward on their snouts and by their big mouths studded with sharp teeth. It is believed that some morays are venomous.

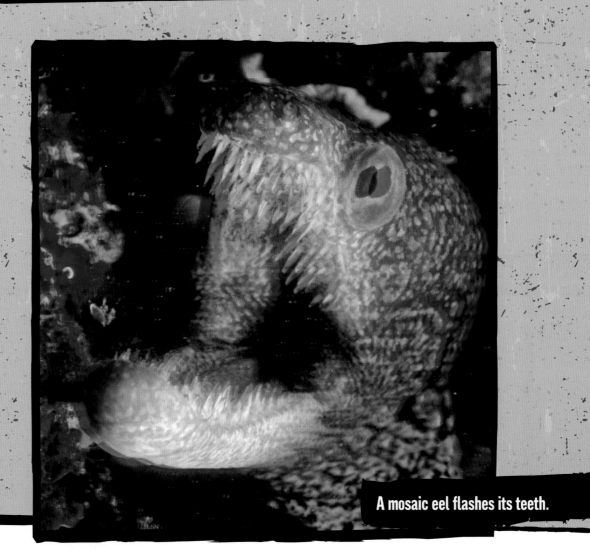

A mosaic eel flashes its teeth.

Jaws within Jaws

Morays have a special feature perfectly suited to their role as predators. Past their jaws, down their throats, morays have a second set of jaws, called pharyngeal (fer-IN-jee-ul) jaws. A moray grabs its prey with its regular jaws. Then, its pharyngeal jaws move forward, snap on the prey, and drag it down the moray's throat.

Ribbons

This green eel displays a dorsal fin that extends the length of its body. Morays are known for their long, ribbonlike dorsal fins.

Green eels are covered by a layer of mucus that protects them from parasites. This is what gives green eels their distinctive color.

Giant Morays

The giant moray is not the longest moray eel, but it is the heaviest. It can weigh 80 pounds (36 kg). Giant morays live in the tropical waters of the Indo-Pacific region. They have large teeth and can inflict painful bites.

Giant morays have been known to attack scuba divers.

THAT'S WILD

SCIENTIFIC NAMES: Mosaic moray: *Enchelycore ramosa,* Green moray: *Gymnothorax funebris,* Giant moray: *Gymnothorax javanicus*

LENGTH: Mosaic moray: 6 ft. (1.8 m), Green moray: 7.5 ft. (2.3 m), Giant moray: 10 ft. (3 m)

LOCATION: tropical and subtropical waters around the world

MOSQUITO

The mosquito is the most dangerous animal on Earth. Mosquitoes don't eat people, or at least not more than a drop of blood at a time, and they're not venomous. Instead, mosquitoes' deadly danger comes from the diseases they inject into their victims. Mosquito-borne illnesses kill millions of people around the world every year. That's many, many thousands of times more than the number of deaths caused by all the other animals in this book combined.

THAT'S WILD

SCIENTIFIC NAME: There are about 3,500 species of mosquito, all in the family *Culicidae*

SIZE: Up to .5 inch (1.3 cm) long

LOCATION: tropical and subtropical regions around the world; some species in cooler climates

Tiny Vampire

Only female mosquitoes suck blood. They need it in order for their eggs to develop. The female homes in on her meal with senses that detect the heat, carbon dioxide (CO_2), and water vapor given off by her victim's skin. The mosquito stabs through the skin with her saw-tipped, double-barreled snout. One tube sucks out the blood, while the other injects saliva that keeps the blood from clotting. The saliva makes the mosquito bite itch. It can also carry parasites and germs that cause malaria, yellow fever, West Nile virus, and other diseases.

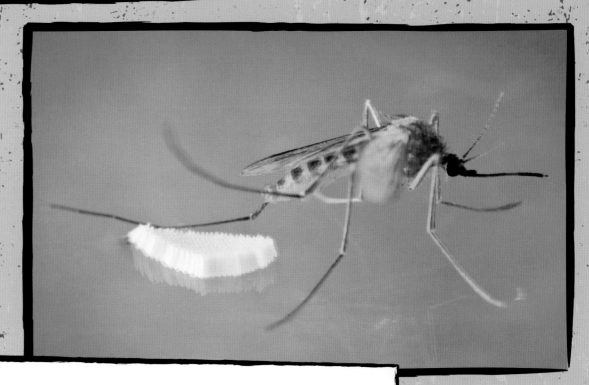

Water Birth

Mosquitoes lay their eggs in still water. Bristly, wormlike larvae hatch from the eggs. The larvae live in the water, eating tiny microbes before becoming pupae and transforming into winged adults.

NILE CROCODILE

The Nile crocodile, a creature that has changed little in the last 200 million years, will attack and eat just about anything that crosses its path: fish, turtles, and birds, as well as large mammals (even people). Nile crocs drag their prey into the water and roll over to drown it. Crocs don't chew their meals—they tear off chunks and swallow them whole.

A Nile crocodile snaps at a wildebeest traveling across a river.

THAT'S WILD

SCIENTIFIC NAME: *Crocodylus niloticus*

LENGTH: 16 feet (5 m)

WEIGHT: 500 lbs. (225 kg)

LOCATION: sub-Saharan Africa

Croc or Gator?

Crocodiles and alligators are closely related animals and look similar, but there are some simple ways to tell them apart. Seen from above, a croc's snout is more V-shaped, and an alligator's is more U-shaped. And because a croc's upper and lower jaws are the same width, its teeth interlock when its mouth is closed. (An alligator's lower teeth aren't visible when its mouth is closed.) In this photo, you can see the indentation in the croc's upper jaw where the fourth lower tooth slides into place when the jaws are closed.

Not Very Social

Nile crocodiles aren't very social animals, but they do work together during feeding by blocking rivers to trap fish and supporting one another when tearing off bites from large prey. And they don't mind sunning themselves in groups.

ORANGUTAN

Orangutans are muscular great apes. They sleep in trees, as high as 100 feet (30 m) above the ground, building new nests almost every evening. They are powerful and intelligent animals, known to make and use tools.

ENDANGERED

Special Males

Some adult male orangutans—described as flanged (FLANJD)—develop special features that females appear to prefer in mates. Flanged males have broad ridges on their faces, known as cheek pads, and a throat sack hanging under their chins. Flanged males make long, loud calls to attract mates.

This flanged male is displaying his cheek pads, throat sack, and impressive teeth.

In the Trees

Orangutans spend almost all their time in trees. Their bodies are well adapted for their arboreal (ar-BOR-ee-ul), or tree-dwelling, lives. Their long hands with opposable thumbs and feet with opposable big toes are useful for grabbing and hanging on to branches. Their shoulder and hip joints are very flexible. This makes it easy for orangutans to climb trees and swing from branch to branch.

THAT'S WILD

SCIENTIFIC NAME:
Pongo pygmaeus (in Borneo) and *Pongo abelii* (in Sumatra)

SIZE: Height: 5 ft. (1.5 m); arm span: 8 ft. (2.4 m)

WEIGHT: 300 lbs. (135 kg) for males; females weigh about half this

LOCATION: Borneo and Sumatra

Orangutans are the largest arboreal animals in the world.

POLAR BEAR

The polar bear is the world's largest land predator. With its all-white camouflage, sharp teeth, and raking claws, the bear is a deadly hunter on the Arctic ice.

On the Hunt

Seals are polar bears' favorite food. Most often, the bear hunts by lying in wait at the edge of the water or beside a hole in the ice. When a seal comes up to breathe, the bear bites down on its head and flips the seal up onto the ice to be eaten. If a seal is already out of the water, lying on the ice, the bear will stalk closer, then break into a sudden, deadly charge. With a top speed of 25 mph (40 kph), a running polar bear can snag a seal with teeth or claws before the prey reaches the water. Sometimes the bear attacks from the other direction, rushing up out of the water to grab an unsuspecting seal.

THAT'S WILD

SCIENTIFIC NAME: *Ursus maritimus*

SIZE: 8.5 ft. (2.6 m)

WEIGHT: 1,200 lbs. (540 kg)

LOCATION: the Arctic

Polar bears wander as far as 40 miles (64 km) each day in search of food. They travel far from land, swimming or jumping between drifting ice floes.

Polar bears spend most of their time alone, coming together only to mate. Males fight with each other to compete for mates.

SPOTTED HYENA

Hyenas look a bit like dogs, but they're more closely related to cats. The spotted hyena is the largest hyena species. This African hunter and scavenger will eat almost any animal it can catch or find, large or small. In places where hyenas live near humans, they will scavenge garbage and sometimes kill livestock. They rarely attack people.

Spotted hyenas have long necks, powerful jaws, and the sharp teeth of a meat eater.

THAT'S WILD

SCIENTIFIC NAME: *Crocuta crocuta*

SIZE: 3 ft. (.9 m)

WEIGHT: 150 lbs. (68 kg)

LOCATION: sub-Saharan Africa

Hyenas have a reputation as scavengers, but they are actually skilled hunters. As much as 95 percent of their food is killed by the hyenas themselves.

Hyena Clans

Hyenas live in groups called clans. A clan can have as few as a handful of hyenas or as many as 90. The clan leader is a female, and all the females in the group are dominant (that is, bosses of the males). The clan breaks up into smaller groups to hunt and forage for food. Hyenas are pack hunters. They work together to cut an animal like an antelope or a zebra out of its herd, and then chase it down for the kill. They will even work as a group to drive a lion away from its own kill to claim it for themselves. When a large animal is killed, the whole clan will get together to eat it.

WESTERN DIAMONDBACK RATTLESNAKE

About 7,000 people are bitten by venomous snakes in the United States every year. Of those bites, about 15 are fatal. The western diamondback rattlesnake is responsible for many of them.

A rattler usually keeps its fangs folded up against the roof of its mouth. But when the mouth opens to strike, the fangs flip down like switchblades. They're sharp, hollow tubes, like hypodermic needles to inject deadly venom.

THAT'S WILD

SCIENTIFIC NAME: *Crotalus atrox*

LENGTH: 7 ft. (2 m)

LOCATION: southwestern United States and northern Mexico

Pit Viper

The diamondback has a pair of pitlike depressions in its face, in front of and slightly below the eyes. All snakes in the group called pit vipers have them. The pits are heat-detecting organs. The snake uses them to zero in on warm-blooded prey, such as mice.

The western diamondback is the second-largest rattlesnake in the United States. This large viper can be recognized by its fat body, triangular head, the dark diamond pattern on its back, and, of course, the warning sound of the rattle that gives the snake its name.

Warning Rattle

The diamondback shakes the rattle on its tail as a warning when it feels threatened. It's for the snake's own protection, to keep it from being stepped on or injured by other animals. The rattle is made of hollow, locked-together segments of keratin, the same material fingernails are made of. A new segment is added to the rattle every time the snake sheds its skin.

WOLVERINE

The fierce wolverine looks like a small, humpbacked bear, but it's really the largest land-dwelling member of the weasel family. Only the sea otter is bigger.

Meat Lover

Wolverines are mostly meat eaters, going after any kind of meat they can get. They are both scavengers and hunters, depending on the season and availability of food. Moose, elk, and deer are their biggest sources of food. Most of these are carcasses killed by wolves or other predators, or animals that have died during the winter. But wolverines also attack and kill even large prey on their own. They scavenge or hunt animals of all kinds, including birds, fish, rodents, predators, whales, and seals that wash up on the beach——and even other wolverines.

A wolverine's jaws and teeth are strong enough to crunch through the meat and bones of a moose carcass in the dead of winter, when it's frozen solid.

Traveler

Wolverines travel long distances in search of food, as far as 20 miles (32 km) in a single day, sometimes moving right over the tops of mountains.

THAT'S WILD

SCIENTIFIC NAME: *Gulo gulo*

SIZE: 3 ft. (.9 m), nose to tail

WEIGHT: 40 lbs. (18 kg)

LOCATION: northern North America, Europe, and Asia

Wolverines' huge, wide feet make it easy for them to walk on snow.

 DANGER!

ANIMAL	DANGER RATING	DANGEROUS FEATURES
Moray eel	51	Sharp teeth, second set of jaws
Orangutan	59	Hands, feet, teeth, strength, intelligence
Wolverine	61	Jaws, teeth, claws, ferocity
Black widow	62	Deadly bite
Gray wolf	65	Jaws, teeth, pack hunting
Spotted hyena	65	Jaws, teeth, pack hunting
Western diamondback rattlesnake	70	Size, deadly venom
Jaguar	72	Jaws, teeth, claws, stealth
Komodo dragon	73	Claws, teeth, infection, speed
Deathstalker scorpion	73	Fatal sting
Chimpanzee	73	Hands, feet, teeth, strength, intelligence
Polar bear	73	Jaws, teeth, claws, size
African elephant	73	Tusks, trunk, feet, size, charging attack
King cobra	75	Size, speed, deadly venom
Grizzly bear	82	Jaws, teeth, claws, speed, strength
Bengal tiger	86	Jaws, teeth, claws, stealth
Lion	87	Jaws, teeth, claws, speed, coordinated attacks
Cape buffalo	89	Deadly horns, nasty temper
Great white shark	90	Jaws, teeth, speed
Hippopotamus	92	Machete-like teeth, ramming attacks
Nile crocodile	94	Crushing jaws, ambush attacks
Mosquito	98	Carries deadly diseases